Do You Understand Me?

Sofie Koborg Brøsen

Jessica Kingsley Publishers
London and Philadelphia

of related interest

How To Be Yourself in a World That's Different
An Asperger's Syndrome Study Guide for Adolescents
Yuko Yoshida M.D.
Foreword by Lorna Wing
Translated by Esther Sanders
ISBN 978 1 84310 504 6

All Cats Have Asperger Syndrome
Kathy Hoopmann
ISBN 978 1 84310 481 0

Autism and Me
Rory Hoy
ISBN 978 1 84310 546 6

Autistic Planet
Jennifer Elder
Illustrated by Marc Thomas and Jennifer Elder
ISBN 978 1 84310 842 9

Everyday Education
Visual Support for Children with Autism
Pernille Dyrbjerg and Maria Vedel
Foreword by Lennart Pedersen
ISBN 978 1 84310 457 5

Brotherly Feelings
Me, My Emotions, and My Brother with Asperger's Syndrome
Sam Frender and Robin Schiffmiller
Illustrated by Dennis Dittrich
ISBN 978 1 84310 850 4

Mind Reading
The Interactive Guide to Emotions - Version 1.3
Simon Baron-Cohen
ISBN 978 1 84310 559 6
ISBN 978 1 84310 560 2

First published in Danish as Kan I Forstå Mig?
in 2005 by the Videnscenter for Autisme

First published in English in 2006
by Jessica Kingsley Publishers
116 Pentonville Road
London N1 9JB, UK
and
400 Market Street, Suite 400
Philadelphia, PA 19106, USA

www.jkp.com

Copyright © Sofie Koborg Brøsen 2006
Translation by Michael Ford
Graphics by Kasper Kruse and Karlsson2/
Illustrations by Peter Brøsen

Library of Congress Cataloging in Publication Data
Koborg Brøsen, Sofie.
   [Kan i forstå mig? English]
   Do you understand me? : my life, my thoughts, my autism spectrum disorder / Sofie
Koborg Brøsen.
      p. cm.
   "First published in Danish as Kan i forstå mig? in 2005 by the Videnscenter for
Autisme"--T.p. verso.
   ISBN-13: 978-1-84310-464-3 (pbk. : alk. paper)
   ISBN-10: 1-84310-464-4 (pbk. : alk. paper) 1. Koborg Brøsen, Sofie--Juvenile literature.
2. Autistic children--Denmark--Biography--Juvenile literature. I. Title.
   RJ506.A9K6213 2006
   618.92'858820092--dc22
   [B]

                                                      2006008438

British Library Cataloguing in Publication Data
A CIP catalogue record for this book is available from the British Library

ISBN 978 1 84310 464 3

Printed and bound in Great Britain by
Athenaeum Press, Gateshead, Tyne and Wear

I have a disability. It's called autism or Asperger Syndrome. You can't see it. It's something I'm born with that I can't help. It means that I find it difficult to understand other people, because they do not think like I do.

I would like to help other people. Sometimes I need help myself. I want other people to understand my life, so that they can understand me.

I prefer things to be the same every day. Every morning, I follow my checklist on the fridge. Then I know what to do. I get easily confused, if I don't know what I'm going to do. Or if I'm going to do things I haven't done before. I need things to be explained to me in advance.

I watch children's television every day at five o'clock in the afternoon. It's hard for me to tell the time. If my mum forgets to tell me that it's five o'clock, and I'm late for my cartoons, I get very cross. If it's only a movie with real people in it, I don't get so cross.

I have a chart in the living room with a drawing and words telling me how the remote control works. I've tried to learn how to use it for years now.

It makes me angry when there are things other children can easily do that I can't.

I WOULD LIKE SOME... UHM...
I CAN'T REMEMBER WHAT THEY ARE CALLED. RAWSTERRIES? BERRYSTEMS? STRAWBUNS?
JORDBÆR
DANSKE
DANSKE
10,-

I can't always find the right words when I have to, and that really makes me sad and annoyed. I often find it difficult to remember the names of people and things.

It's also difficult to find words to describe what things are like. I think it's difficult to explain how I feel. I prefer short conversations.

I can't remember all the names of the children in my form. I still don't know all the names of my teachers. I know all the names of almost every single cartoon character because that's a lot easier for me.

Mum says I speak somewhat differently than other people. Sometimes I use sentences from cartoons and comic strips without even knowing it.

Sometimes my mum laughs at me and then I get a little cross with her. Mum says she isn't laughing at me. She is laughing at what I say, and it's only because she cares so much about me. But I feel stupid when other people are laughing.

Mum says that I sometimes speak as if I were a grown-up. It sounds as if I want to order people around or educate them. I can't hear how I speak. I think I speak quite normally all of the time.

I get confused if people ask me to do several things at once. I like being told what to do one step at a time.

If the teachers say a lot of things all at once, then I just draw pictures until they come and explain to me what we're supposed to do.

When too much is going on at once, I feel stressed. If there's too much noise, I leave the classroom.

I find it very hard to see which way to pass people when they are walking towards me. I always expect them to keep going straight ahead, but sometimes they don't.

Mum says that it's because other people get confused or annoyed, because I don't use body language. I find it hard to see body language.

Mum says that other people can't tell what I want, because I don't use many facial expressions. Others might think I'm angry or sad when I'm fine.

I can't tell from people's faces if they are joking or lying. I believe that everything other people tell me is the truth. I also think it's very difficult to understand jokes.

It helps me a lot if people say things to me in a straightforward manner. They shouldn't use a lot of confusing words and sentences. They should use words that mean exactly what they want to say.

I have support lessons in school. I like that. I'm good at languages, but I find maths and science extremely difficult.

When the other girls say I'm good at reading and writing, and that I'll probably become a writer, it makes me very happy.

The best teacher at my school is Ida. I feel safe when I see her, and she is nice to me.

Ida always has time for me. Ida is calm and good at explaining things to me in a way that I understand. If I'm crying and feeling sad, she helps me.

Before I got my support teacher, I couldn't do physical education. I got confused all the time. I like physical education when my support teacher is there.

Mum says I'm stubborn because I'm not very good at changing my mind. That's why group work is difficult for me. If we are working on projects or in groups, I prefer to have my support teacher there.

I like going to the library and the swimming baths. I love music. I adore Elvis and Peruvian panpipes.

I have trouble following what the other children at school are doing. I can't always understand the rules of their games. I often think that they just don't care for me. Then I get upset and don't care for them either.

Some of the other children get together in groups and find someone to tease. Usually, I'm the one they tease. Then I feel as if I'm going to be sick.

I think it's difficult to understand other children because they seem very unnatural. At school it's mostly the younger children who want to be with me. I sometimes read to them.

I would like to play with the children in my form. I wish they would sometimes ask me. I don't know how to ask them in a way to get them to say yes.

I usually keep to myself.

Whenever I do play with the girls from my form, I'm very happy.

It's difficult for me to be with a lot of people at the same time. I prefer being with one person at a time. I like to be with children who are quiet and calm.

Usually it doesn't matter when the other children are noisy – just not when I'm reading. Then I lose my temper and shout to make them shut up.

There is someone else at school, Lisa, with whom I sometimes play. She is in the form above me.
The others in her form sometimes think she is a bit strange but I think Lisa is very natural and very nice.

Lisa is my best friend.

I wish everyone could be like Lisa and me. I don't like it when other people swear and talk rudely about each other. Lisa and I don't.

I think a lot about what the other children are like.

The girls are interested in boys as boyfriends. I'm not interested in boys – only to play with.

Some of the girls wear bras, even when they don't have to. I think that's silly.

The girls write in their diaries. So do I. But there's also a boy who uses a diary. He's not like the other boys. He's calmer and he doesn't swear as much as they do.

Some girls and boys are not like other boys and girls. It's difficult to understand.

My timetable often confuses me.

Mum and I have an arrangement, and I call her every day when school's over. I always have my mobile phone with me. Then mum tells me if I'm calling too soon.

Sometimes the other children in my form have gone to the music hall or to the arts and crafts hall without me noticing it. Then I think we're off for the day and I pack my school bag and call my mum. Then mum says that she'll come and pick me up, or she tells me if I've forgotten to go to more lessons, which don't take place in our classroom.

Sometimes the girls in my form accompany me to the right place. I like that so much.

I like reading, so I spend most of my time at the library. I read comic books as often as I can. I think I've read every single comic book in the school library. I also read a lot of other books. I prefer modern fairytales like Harry Potter.

Mum calls me a bookworm, but I don't like the word worm. It makes me feel sick. I asked mum to call me a bookkeeper instead.

Words such as brain and bowels and slime also make me feel sick. The doctor has models of the internal parts of the human body. When I look at them, I feel like vomiting.

I don't like the idea of people having horrible things like that inside them.

I think it's strange that the sign on the door at the doctors says "open", when the door is actually closed!

Once a teacher said to me, "get your skates on". I thought we were going skating, but she meant that I should hurry up.

I get angry with myself when I don't understand things. It makes me happy when other people say things, so that I can understand them.

One day one of the girls in my form said to me, "We're just joking, Sofie, you can take it!" She laughed and smiled a very nice smile when she said it. That meant she wasn't teasing. It helped a lot that she said it.

I'm not very good when it comes to traffic. I can't read a map, and I don't know which way to go.

I don't like it when things are too difficult, or if problems arise that I can't solve.

I also have to be more careful with strangers than other children. I can't tell if other people want to hurt me or not, and that can be dangerous.

My mum takes me to school and picks me up – every day. Mum says that when I go to secondary school, I'll perhaps be able to learn to take the bus on my own.

I sometimes get things wrong. Mum and I were in a shop – I saw a purse and asked her if I could have it. Mum answered my question in a way that made me think I could.

I put the purse on the counter with the other stuff. Mum didn't find out until after we'd paid and had left the shop. Mum hadn't said that I could have it.

I cried and got upset because I had misunderstood her. Then mum comforted me and bought something for my little brother, which cost the exact same amount of money as the purse. We each had something that cost the same amount of money. And then everything was fine again.

I want things to be fair and for everyone to have the same amount of everything.

I get upset every time I get things wrong, or when other people misunderstand me.

Most of all I love to stay at home and just sit in a chair and read with my feet up. It's particularly nice if my cat, Teddy, is with me and I have something nice to eat and drink as well.

I feel safe at home. My family is a happy family. We have a swing in the living room where I can go round and round. I turn the fastest because I don't get dizzy.

When other people say something incorrectly, I correct them. Mum's taught me that it's rude to correct grown-ups. But I don't like it when other people make mistakes.

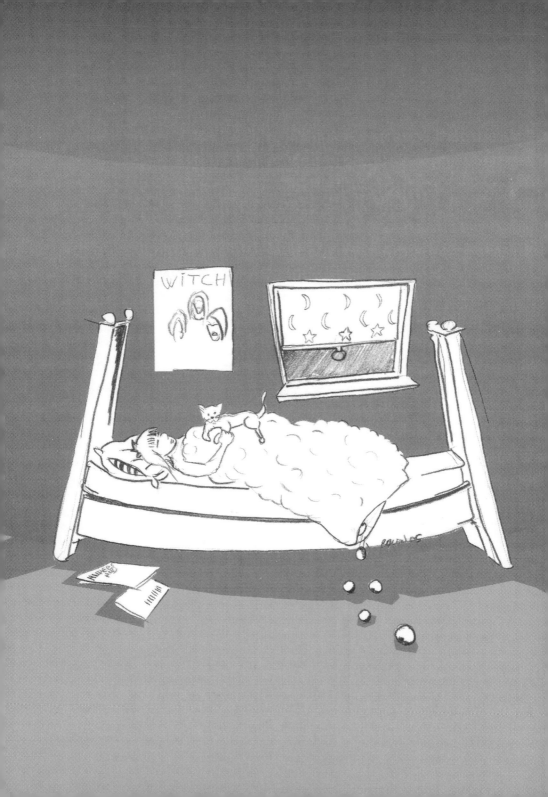

I have a very heavy blanket filled with hollow balls. I need it because my skin doesn't have the same sensitivity as other people's skin. The balls help my skin to feel the way it should.

Before I got my ball blanket, I couldn't stand it if anyone sat too close to me. Or if someone touched me and I wasn't prepared for it.

I sometimes hit people, without meaning to, if they touched me, because it felt really bad. I prefer soft clothes I can't feel that I'm wearing. A lot of clothes annoy my skin.

I also get really annoyed by strong light and smells. Certain sounds and certain smells hurt me. Then I try to get away, so I can concentrate again.

I like going to the beach and on picnics. I think nature is really beautiful, and I don't like ugly, grey houses. There are too many houses in towns.

I love beautiful things, and I've collected a lot of treasures. I've chosen some pretty, white furniture for my room. I prefer things to be neat and tidy always.

Twice a year mum takes me to camp. We meet a lot of other families who have children with autism.

I have a lot of friends at camp. They understand me, I understand them, and for the most part we agree. We play and nobody teases you. We eat delicious meals and have homemade cakes every day.

Last time we made a funny movie. I played a bad-tempered aunt. It was fun.

I always get really sad and upset when we have to leave and go home. Then I look forward to the next camp.

I often dream that I'm in my own little world.

Sometimes I visit my granny. Then I get to take a bath in her tub – and I dream of Greece.

At my grandparents' house there's a cupboard with sweets for the children. That's so nice. I would like to own their little white house when I grow up.

The very best thing about my cat, Teddy, is that he is always quiet and calm. Teddy is my second best friend.

I find cats a lot easier to understand than people. I want to run a boarding house for cats when I grow up. But I probably can't support myself doing that.

I look forward to growing old and retiring. Then I'll live in a little white house in the country and have lots of cats. And I'll stay home every day and take care of my cats.

Sometimes I wish I didn't have autism.

But I still like myself the way I am.

Can I tell you about Asperger Syndrome?
A Guide for Friends and Family

Jude Welton
Illustrated by Jane Telford
Foreword by Elizabeth Newson
48 pages ISBN 978 1 84310 206 9 pb

'This is an excellent resource for anybody who may come into contact with AS and I believe parents of children with this condition should be guided to this volume before seeking answers on the internet or elsewhere.'

– *The Frontline of Learning Disability*

'This book packs a lot of wisdom and information into a small package.'

– *Autism Coach Website*

'Parents have needed this book for a very long time.'

– *Elizabeth Newson, Early Years Diagnostic Centre*

Meet Adam – a young boy with AS. Adam helps children understand the difficulties faced by a child with AS – he tells them what AS is, what it feels like to have AS and how they can help children with AS by understanding their differences and appreciating their talents. This illustrated book is ideally suited for boys and girls between 7 and 15 years old and also serves as a superb starting point for family and classroom discussions.

Jude Welton has a 10-year-old son with AS. Although originally trained as a child psychologist specializing in autism, she is a freelance writer, writing mainly on the arts. She recently started writing about and for children with AS.

Jessica Kingsley Publishers
www.jkp.com